Peace
of Heart

Series Preface

The volumes in NCP's "7 x 4" series offer a meditation a day for four weeks, a bite of food for thought, a reflection that lets a reader ponder the spiritual significance of each and every day. Small enough to slip into a purse or coat pocket, these books fit easily into everyday routines.

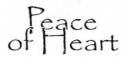

Peace of Heart

Reflections on Choices in Daily Life

Marc Foley

New City Press
Hyde Park, New York

In gratitude to my friend
Sandra Gettings
for her wise suggestions on the text.

Published in the United States by New City Press
202 Cardinal Rd., Hyde Park, NY 12538
www.newcitypress.com
©2008 New City Press

Cover design by Durva Correia

Library of Congress Cataloging-in-Publication Data:

Foley, Marc, 1949-
    Peace of heart : reflections on choices in daily life / Marc Foley.
        p. cm. -- ("7 x 4" : A meditation a day for a span of four weeks)
    Includes bibliographical references.
    ISBN 978-1-56548-293-7 (pbk. : alk. paper) 1. Peace of mind--
Religious aspects--Christianity--Meditations. I. Title.

BV4908.5.F65 2008
242--dc22   2007052928

Printed in the United States of America

Contents

three
The Peace
of Charity

four
Being at Peace
with Oneself

Foreword

When Rabbi Joshua Liebman was a young man, he made a list of the things that he believed would bring him happiness. The list was extensive; it included, among other things, love, health, and fame. Liebman shared his list with a wise old man who replied that his list lacked an essential ingredient for happiness — Peace of Mind. Without it, explained the old man, a person can never be happy because even if he possesses all the goods of this earth, without peace of mind, he would possess them with an unhappy heart.

But how can we achieve peace of mind? We can only experience it truly when we have true peace of soul: when we are in right relationship with God, our neighbor, and our deepest self. Let us explore how small practices and daily choices can foster true peace of soul.

Staying Rooted in God's Presence

The Great Principle

"The great principle of the interior life lies in peace of heart," writes De Caussade. "It must be preserved with such care that the moment it is in danger, everything else should be abandoned for its re-establishment.... The reason for this is that peace and tranquility of spirit alone give the soul great strength to achieve all that God wills."[1]

We lose our peace of soul when we lose our awareness of God's presence. It is re-established when we re-center our mind upon God. There are many means by which we can accomplish this task. For example, we can simply close our eyes for a moment and focus on God's indwelling presence; we can look at a picture or read a saying that re-centers our mind upon God, or we can repeat a favorite line of Scripture or poetry that we have committed to memory. What practice helps you to return to the Shepherd and Guardian of your soul?

Where Will You Live Today?

Our mind is a vast universe of thoughts; our consciousness an endless stream of images and emotionally laden ideas that we cannot stop. We cannot shut down our fretful minds, but we can choose what ideas we focus upon. An old Chinese proverb says, "That the birds of worry and care fly over your head, this you cannot change, but that they built nests in your hair, this you can prevent."

The wisdom of the proverb lies in differentiating between what we can do from what we can't do. To expect that we can stop worry from circling around our minds is unrealistic. In fact, trying to stop it only makes matters worse, for we give power to the things we resist. Attempting *not* to think of something is to focus upon it. Try to be at peace with this reality.

But we are not powerless. We can prevent our thoughts from building nests in our hair. That is, we can choose what thoughts we dwell upon. We can brood upon past hurts and injuries or allow our minds to run wild with worry about every fearful possibility that the future may have in store for us. Or we can gently focus our mind on God's Eternal Presence dwelling within us, realizing that we can never be alone, never separated from the One who loves us. "The mind is its own place," wrote John Milton, "and in itself can make a Heav'n of Hell and a Hell of Heav'n."[2] What place will you live in today?

First Thoughts Upon Awakening

3

When we awake in the morning, our minds are often assaulted by anxious thoughts and images about the tasks that lie before us, the unfinished business heaped up upon our desks, financial worries, sickness, worries of all sorts. If we dwell upon these thoughts, we will lose our peace of soul because we have lost all sense of God's presence. To prevent this from happening, we need to attend to God's guidance as we arise from sleep. De Caussade writes, "We should pay attention to what strikes us most forcibly at the beginning of the day, and to what God's grace inclines our hearts, pondering over it quietly."[3]

Ponder quietly the eternal truths that God awakens within you at the beginning of the day: be it that God loves you; that God has endowed you with an immortal soul, or that God will guide you throughout the darkest night. And allow this thought to incline your heart. This will sustain your peace of soul, for it will anchor you in God's presence.

Last Thoughts Upon Falling Asleep 4

When Mozart was thirty-one years old, he wrote the following to his father Leopold: "I have made acquaintance during these last few years with [death], this best and truest friend of mankind, so that his image not only no longer has any terrors for me, but suggests much that is reassuring and consoling! And I thank my God for blessing me with the opportunity of coming to recognize Him as the key of our true blessedness. I never lie down upon my bed without reflecting that, young as I am, I may perhaps never see another day, and yet not one of those who know me can say that I am morose or sad among my fellows! For this blessing I daily thank my Creator and wish with all my heart that my fellow-men may share it."[4]

Mozart's experience is not unique. For centuries, spiritual writers have suggested that we meditate upon our mortality as a means of overcoming the listlessness and dullness of daily life. The word mundane, derived from the Latin *mundus*, means worldly. And life becomes mundane when we cannot see beyond this world. Thoughts of death remind us that there is an Eternal world beyond our own — the key of our true blessedness.

So as you lay your head upon your pillow, ponder that you may never see another day. And if you awake the next morning, you will be more aware of God who stands at the threshold of the new day.

Getting Ready for the Day

Many of us dread going to work because we know that we will have to deal with someone who aggravates us or challenges our patience daily. Is there anything that can help us to retain our peace of soul in this situation? Shakespeare offers us some advice through one of his characters. In *Henry V*, as King Henry is about to lead his army into battle, he says to his men, "All things are ready if our minds be so."[5] If we prepare ourselves mentally before we have to deal with an exasperating co-worker, we can retain our peace of soul.

There was a nun in the Carmelite convent of Lisieux who grated on everyone's nerves. When one of St. Thérèse's novices confessed that she had failed to be kind to this nun in spite of her good resolutions, Thérèse responded, "If you are easily overcome, it is because you do not soften your heart in advance. When you are exasperated with someone, the way to recover your peace of mind is to pray for that person."[6]

There are two reasons why prayer helps us to retain our peace of soul. First, it softens our heart toward the person who aggravates us. Second, it grounds us in the presence of God. Is there any better way to prepare for the day?

Charity, the Very Life of God

6

Many people believe that their lives are meaningless because their tasks are dull and their work makes no contribution to society. But no life is worthless, no matter how insignificant it may seem, for every person has the capacity to be a sacrament of God's presence in this world.

We speak of performing "common" acts of charity. But there is nothing common about love, for charity is the very life of God. As St. Thomas Aquinas writes, "Since the divine essence is charity ... the charity by which we love our neighbor is a sharing in the divine charity."[7] In short, when we love, we share in the very life of God and communicate that life to those around us. We make a dreadful mistake when we judge the worth of our lives on the basis of the tasks that we perform. What greater meaning can life hold than to share the very life of God with others?

7 An Eternal Perspective

Philadelphia won the sixth and deciding game of the 1980 World Series when Tug McGraw struck out Kansas City's Willie Wilson in the bottom of the ninth inning with the bases loaded. After this tense game, a newspaper reporter asked McGraw how he stood up under the pressure of knowing that his performance could have determined the outcome of the series. McGraw said that a strange thing happened to him as he was standing on the pitcher's mound. An uncanny peace descended upon him as he realized that in a billion years when the sun had burnt out and our world had been covered over with ice, that how he pitched on that particular day would make no difference.

Seeing the events of time against the backdrop of eternity helps us to *live* in the present moment and prevents us from becoming *absorbed* in it. An eternal perspective allows us to see all things in their true light. The realization that all things come to an end does not diminish the significance of our work; it merely helps us to respond to it proportionally. How often do we expend a hundred dollars of emotional energy on a ten cent issue?

To retain our peace of soul, we need the perspective that we find in St. Teresa of Avila's bookmark: "Let nothing trouble you. Let nothing frighten you. All things are passing. God never changes. Patience obtains all things. God alone suffices."

Perhaps Tug McGraw won the game because he was at peace — the peace that came from realizing that if he had lost the World Series, his world would not have come to an end.

An Eternal Perspective

two

Beauty: The Countenance of God

In his book, *Mozart, Traces of Transcendence,* Hans Küng argues that some passages in Mozart's music have such sublime beauty that they are nothing less than intimations of God. This statement should not take us by surprise, for beauty has always been considered a transcendental property of Being, the visible splendor of Truth and Goodness. It is no wonder that the great sixth century mystic Pseudo-Dionysius wrote that Beauty is one of God's chief attributes and that "beauty is the cause of harmony, of sympathy and community."[8]

All of us have felt the truth of this statement. Who among us has not listened to music, contemplated a great piece of art, read a masterpiece of world literature or stood in an open field on a tranquil morning and felt a deep harmony and sympathy with all God's creatures?

In the *Paradiso,* when Dante sees creation *sub specie aeternitatis,* in the light of eternity, he is awakened to the reality that the universe is the seamless garment of God. Aesthetic experiences do not remove us from this world; rather they disclose to us the mind of God. Each day, pause and allow yourself to be nourished by what God's creation discloses to you.

2 Beauty and Goodness

St. John of the Cross writes that a grace received in the past is still operative in the memory and should be called to mind as often as it aids in "a renewal of love and an elevation of the mind to God."[9] We find an expression of this truth in the life of the poet William Wordsworth.

In July, 1798, William Wordsworth toured the Wye Valley in Wales, renowned for its beauty. The visit left a profound effect upon his soul. In his poem *Tintern Abbey,* Wordsworth states that whenever he recalled the beauty that he had seen, it had the power to soften his heart and incline his will to be kind.

> Though absent long,
> These forms of beauty have not been to me,
> As is a landscape to a blind man's eye:
> But oft, in lonely rooms, and mid the din
> Of towns and cities, I have owed to them,
> In hours of weariness, sensations sweet,
> … perhaps,

As may have had no trivial influence
On that best portion of a good man's life;
His little, nameless, unremembered acts
Of kindness and of love.[10]

What past graces recorded in your memory, recalled to mind, have the power to soften your heart toward your neighbor and incline your will to be kind? Can anything bring us more peace than having a kind heart?

3 Nothing Lasts Forever

In *Frank and Maise: A Memoir with Parents,* Wilfred Sheed writes that his parents Frank Sheed and Maise Ward immensely enjoyed their work, operating their publishing house, because they took for granted that it would not last forever. They took their work seriously because they knew that it was of God. But they worked in such a light-hearted way that it can be said they personified St. Augustine's saying, "Do everything as though it were the most important act in the world, but also as though you were going to die the next minute and it didn't make any difference."

Each of us needs this perspective. Our lives are important because we are called to do God's work, whatever that may be. Yet, we should undertake our work with a light-heartedness because we can die tomorrow.

Pondering the temporality of life discloses
the significance of the present moment.

On Route

St. Thérèse fostered the awareness of the presence of God in her life by "proceeding slowly," as one of Thérèse's novices once put it. Whenever Thérèse was going from place to place, she would not rush, but would pace herself. This simple practice kept her aware of God's presence. When we do something consciously, we become conscious of why we do it.

How often in our daily lives are we en route, whether commuting to work or walking from place to place? Getting up from your desk and walking to the file cabinet in the next room can be a mere task or a spiritual exercise. The choice is yours. Proceed slowly. It might take you an extra five seconds to get to the file cabinet, but you will be more at peace when you arrive because you will have been conscious of God's presence en route.

Tomorrow, when you are driving to work, ease up on the accelerator a fraction of a centimeter; slow your normal speed by 1 M.P.H. You will get to work on time and in a more peaceful state of mind because you will be conscious of God's presence en route.

5 Seek and You Will Find

In the business world, a manager will often focus on what is going wrong, who is incompetent or who is wasting time. The emphasis is on correcting mistakes. Ken Blanchard in *The One Minute Manager* offers an alternate style of management. He recommends that a manager skulk around and try to catch people in the act of doing something right and compliment them on their work. Not only has this managerial style proven to be more effective; it has also made the manager's job more peaceful and enjoyable.

When we live like a manager constantly on the lookout for the faults and failings of others, we rob ourselves of peace because we deprive ourselves of the joy of seeing the goodness of God present in those about us. St. Thérèse offers us an alternative. "When I wish to increase love within me, especially when the devil tries to place before the eyes of my soul the faults of such and such a sister, I hasten to search out her virtues, her good intentions."[11] Because the faults of others can be so glaring, it takes effort to *search out* the presence of God in others, that is, their virtues and good intentions. But the search is worth the effort. There is an increase of love within our hearts. Can anything else bring us more peace?

6 Sit on the Bottom of the Ocean

"Peace I leave with you; my peace I give to you" (Jn 14: 27). It might strike us as strange that Jesus spoke these words at the most anxious time in his life, the night before he died. But there is no contradiction in this, for at the same time we can feel anxious and maintain a sense of peace. The soul is like an ocean during a storm. While waves are raging on the surface, deep down on the bottom, all is still and calm.

This is how it must have been for Jesus the night before he died. He was frightened in the face of his impending death but at peace with himself because he knew that he was doing his Father's will. The same is true with us. How often have we made fearful decisions in life, yet experience a peace beyond understanding because we knew we had done the right thing? At such times, we cannot stop the raging waves of fear; we can only ride out the storm. Sit on the bottom of the ocean; find that place within your soul where God dwells and you are at peace with yourself.

7 Intimations of Immortality

Certain childhood memories fill us with inexplicable joy not because of their content but because of the celestial light in which they are bathed. In this regard, Cardinal Newman wrote the following in his sermon *The Mind of Little Children*: "If we wish to affect a person … we can do no better than appeal to the memory of times past, and above all the memories of childhood. For there is in the infant soul … a discernment of the unseen world in the things that are seen, a realization of what is Sovereign and worthy of adoration … for a child has lately come from God's presence.… The child is but a type of what is at length to be fulfilled in us. Therefore we must not lament that our youthful days are gone — for what we were when we were children is a blessed intimation, given for our comfort, of what God will make of us."[12]

Is there a memory from your childhood that brings you peace? Is there a childhood

haunt inside of you to which are fre-
quently drawn? Has it ever occurred to you
that it is God who is beckoning to you? Take
time and sit with that memory, for it is an
intimation of immortality, an aperture to
Eternity.

The Peace
of Charity

three

Inconveniences

We often guard our time and energy because we believe that we need every moment to accomplish our work. But no matter how many unplanned inconveniences show up at our door, somehow everything seems to get done. To acquire true peace of soul, we need to embrace daily interruptions as part of God's plan for our lives. In this regard, Henri Nouwen once told a story of a research professor who was always complaining about being interrupted in his work, until one day he came to the realization that interruptions *were* his work. This insight changed the professor's life. From that moment on, when students or colleagues showed up unexpectedly at his office, he regarded them as people sent to him by God. There will never be a convenient time to love because love requires a willingness to be inconvenienced.

Expect the Unexpected

Woody Allen once said, "If you want to make God laugh, tell him about your plans." When we tell God our daily plans, he must listen with an impish smile, saying to himself, "That's what you think." What God knows by omniscience; we know by experience. Things never work out the way we plan. It is good to make plans, but not to get too attached to them. The more we insist that the world around us does not intrude upon our well-ordered lives, the more upset we become when it inevitably does.

"The art of living," writes Marcus Aurelius, "is more like wrestling than dancing, for it demands a firm and watchful stance against an unexpected upset."[13] These words contain a two-fold wisdom. First, as noted in a previous reflection, prepare yourself mentally to expect the unexpected. "All things are ready if our minds be so."

Second, adopt the watchful stance of a wrestler. To not be thrown off balance, wrestlers maintain a dual focus. Simultaneously, they keep their eyes on their opponent while focusing on their own center of gravity.

We too need to keep a double focus, to not be thrown by the unexpected interruptions of daily life. As you peer through the pile of work on your desk at your colleague who needs to talk, gently focus on that part of your body where you feel tension mounting. This will help you to be patient. Then pray, "Lord, the tension I feel in my shoulders is a small price to pay for the privilege to love, the purpose for which I was created." We all have different occupations but the same vocation — to love. William Blake sums it up:

> And we are put on earth a little space,
> That we may learn to bear the beams of
> love.[14]

Silent Acts of Love

3

While Oscar Wilde was being led off to prison through a jeering and mocking crowd, a man whom he knew took off his hat and bowed his head. Wilde noticed this gesture and was deeply moved. He wrote, "Men have gone to heaven for smaller things than that. It was in this spirit, and with this mode of love, that the saints knelt down to wash the feet of the poor, or stopped to kiss the leper on the cheek. I have never said one single word to him about what he did. I do not know to the present moment whether he is aware that I was even conscious of his action. It is not a thing for which one can render formal thanks in formal words. I keep it as a secret debt that I am glad to think I can never possibly repay. When wisdom has been profitless to me, philosophy barren, and the proverbs and phrases of those who sought to give me consolation are dust and ashes in my mouth, the memory of that little, lovely, silent act of love has unsealed for me all the wells of pity; brought me out of the bitterness of lonely exile into harmony with the wounded, broken and great heart of the world."[15]

We should not undervalue our silent acts of love. As St. Augustine tells us, "God, through whom petty things do not diminish us."[16] We are like the man who took off his hat and bowed his head. Acts of kindness planted in the memories of others may be the very instrument by which God sustains a fellow creature in life's lonely exile.

Unfelt Love

4

Many believe erroneously that if we really loved God, we would *want* to do God's will. But the opposite is often true. St. Thérèse offered the following perspective to her sister Céline: "What a grace when, in the morning, we feel no courage, no strength to practice virtue.… In one act of love, even *unfelt* love, all is repaired, and Jesus smiles."[17] Thérèse understood that when we have neither the strength nor the desire to do God's will, that any act of love, even *unfelt* love, is more precious in the eyes of God than efforts supported by our feelings.

Have you ever considered that when your physical and emotional strength is at its lowest, the least act of love that you perform is an expression of loving God with your *whole* strength and your *whole* heart? Those moments, when we choose to love in spite of our feelings, are experiences of God's grace operating within us. So, when feeling that we have not even an ounce of love to give we choose to love anyway, we should thank God for the awesome miracle that his grace is accomplishing within us.

What Good Have You Done?

In a letter to his agnostic friend, Robert Bridges, Jesuit poet Gerard Manley Hopkins suggested how to dispose oneself to belief in God. "Now you no doubt take for granted that your coming [to faith] turns on the working of your own mind, influenced or uninfluenced by the minds and reasonings of others…. But I have another counsel open to no objection and yet I think it will be unexpected. It is to give alms. It may be either in money or in other shapes…. I should be bold to say give up to the point of inconvenience…. It changes the whole man, if anything can; not his mind only but the will and everything…. The question to be asked is, 'What good have you done?' "[18]

Hopkins' counsel contains a truth, simple yet profound. Namely, if we want to know God who is love, we must love. Hopkins' advice echoes St. John's teaching: "Everyone who loves … knows God. Whoever does not love does not know God" (1 Jn 4:7). How can you come to know God in your daily life? The answer may be simpler than you think. "What good have you done today?"

On Suffering in Silence 6

The bad thing about having a cold, a headache, a queasy stomach or any other minor ailment is that no single one of them is incapacitating. They don't keep us from going to work; they tag along with us. They are nuisances that fog our minds and make us expend more energy to focus upon our jobs. They can make us irritable and short-tempered. So how should we bear minor ailments? St. Teresa of Avila gave her nuns the following advice: "If you can tolerate light illnesses, don't complain about them. When the sickness is serious, it does the complaining itself. Sisters, consider that you are few, and if one has this habit of complaining, it wears everyone out…. Learn how to suffer a little for love of God without having everyone knowing about it."[19]

When you have a headache, how do you respond if asked, "Hi, how are you?" Do you say, "Fine"? Or do you hold the person hostage for five minutes as you drone on about how horrible you're feeling? Such behavior wears everyone out, including ourselves. Whenever we focus on our misery, we make a big deal out of small ailments.

How different we would be at the end of a day if we learned how to suffer a little for the love of God without everyone knowing about it. We would be more at peace with ourselves had we stayed focused on God's presence dwelling within us and had grown in love of our neighbor.

On Keeping One's Peace When Misjudged

Few things in life that can rob us of our peace more than being misunderstood or misjudged. What can we do to retain our peace during such times? Should we suffer in silence or should we defend ourselves? St. Francis de Sales gives the following sage advice: "When falsely accused, defend yourself calmly for the sake of truth and to avoid scandal; if the accusations still continue, remain quite calm and say no more, for having done your duty to truth, you should also do your duty to humility."[20]

The first thing that St. Francis says is easy to understand. Yes, we should *defend* ourselves, but without being *defensive*. If we speak our truth calmly, we are more likely to remain calm. Besides, blowing up in the face of accusation doesn't do any good; in fact, it is likely to make things worse.

But what does St. Francis mean when he says that after we have defended ourselves

and people still do not accept our explana-
tion, we should discharge our duty to humility by remaining silent? He means that we
need to accept humbly the fact that certain
people in life will not believe the truth no
matter how often or how vehemently we say
it. To continue to defend ourselves in such a
situation is a futile exercise that does nothing
but rob us of our peace. We need to ask for
the grace to remain at peace once we have
said our piece.

Being at Peace
with Oneself

four

On Being Merciful to Oneself

No one is perfect. Even the saints had their faults and failings. But the saints accepted their sins and imperfections with humility and gentleness; this is what gave them peace. After St. Thérèse of Lisieux committed a fault, she felt sad and uneasy but learned to bear her feelings with gentleness until they dissipated. Thérèse would talk to herself as if she were trying to console a frightened child. "'Now little one, this is the price you must pay for your fault' and so I patiently bear with the trial until the little debt is paid."[21] Similarly, St. Francis de Sales admonishes: "One of the best exercises of gentleness is to be patient with ourselves and our imperfections.... We should correct our heart gently and calmly after some fault, treating it with mercy rather than anger."[22] We are to correct our heart with gentleness. If we castigate ourselves with cruelty, we rob ourselves of the peace of God because our rage blinds us to how much God loves us.

We are called to talk to ourselves as a loving parent would speak to a frightened child, for this is how God speaks to us. Do not crush anyone weighed down with guilt, not even the burdened child who lives within your heart.

2 The Peace of Being Forgiven

The fifth step in A.A., the "confessional step," is, "Admit to God, to ourselves and to another human being the exact nature of our wrongs." Bill Wilson writes this about it: "Many in A.A., once agnostic or atheistic, tell us that it was during Step Five that they first actually felt the presence of God. And even those who had faith already often become conscious of God as they never were before. This feeling of being at one with God and man, this emerging from isolation through the open and honest sharing of our terrible burden of guilt, brings us to a resting place … "[23]

Guilt deprives us of a resting place within our own hearts; it makes us feel at odds with ourselves and disconnected from the world around us. Guilt makes us afraid because we believe that God is angry with us. In turn, this fear projects upon God a wrathful countenance. Francis Thompson's poem "The

Hound of Heaven" contains an example of this projection. The speaker's guilt portrays God as a vicious hound pursuing him. But when he stops running away from himself and turns around to face the "Hound," he discovers that it is a product of his own fears. "Is my gloom, after all,/ Shade of His hand, outstretched caressingly?"[24] God's hand is not poised to strike us for our sins but raised in benediction to forgive us. The gloom of our soul that guilt creates is transformed into refreshing shade when we accept God's mercy. But to acquire this resting place within our hearts we need to acknowledge our guilt and seek forgiveness. Do you need to ask someone for forgiveness?

3 Self-Inflicted Wounds

Every effect has a corresponding cause; we reap what we have sown. When we act with kindness, we become kind; when we hate, we become hateful.

Every hateful act is a self-inflicted wound. This is represented in one of Aesop's fables. One day, angry because humans were taking their honey, the bees came to Zeus. They asked for the means to inflict pain upon the humans. Zeus granted their request. He provided them with stingers, but whenever one of them stung a human, the bee died.

Our biting words are like bee stingers. Our neighbor will feel the pain our words cause, but we are the ones truly harmed. Whenever we lash out at others, our own soul is wounded.

The Peace of Forgiving

4

Forgiveness is the inner choice to let go of seething resentment and stop nursing our grudge. To come to peace with ourselves, we need to forgive. If we don't, we risk being consumed by our own bitterness. Dante's *Inferno* presents a symbol of how we can be devoured by an unforgiving spirit. In Canto 33, Count Ugolino and his betrayer, Archbishop Ruggieri, are frozen together up to their necks in ice. Ugolino, situated behind Ruggieri, makes a gruesome meal of his betrayer; he gnaws upon his head and neck. As Dante and Virgil come upon this horror, Ugolino raises his bloodstained mouth from his gory repast, wipes it upon his victim's hair and recounts Ruggieri's betrayal. Re-telling his woe only increases Ugolino's rage. "His eyes narrowed to slits when he was done, and he seized the skull once again between his teeth grinding it as a mastiff grinds a bone."[25] What a gruesome image of what we do to ourselves when we ruminate over past injuries.

Cognitive psychologists say that chronic anger comes not from the hurt we experienced twenty years ago but because of ruminating upon that hurt ever since. Such mental mastication devours our mind and heart. We need to ask God for the grace to forgive *for our own sake*. The alternative is too horrifying to contemplate.

Sadness and Anger

All of us know the sting of being insulted and the almost irresistible urge to hurl back a bitter remark. But when we do, our heart becomes bitter and we lose our peace. St. John Climacus offers the following wisdom: "As the gradual pouring of water on a fire puts out the flame completely, so do the tears of genuine sadness extinguish every flame of anger and irascibility.... One day I saw three monks insulted and humiliated in the same way at the same moment. The first felt he had been cruelly hurt; but managed not to say anything. The second was happy for himself but grieved for the one who had insulted him. The third thought only of the harm suffered by his neighbor, and wept with the most ardent compassion. The first was prompted by fear; the second was urged on by the hope of reward; the third was moved by love."[26]

The sorrow of compassion has the power to dissolve anger and soften our hearts, for it is difficult to remain angry with a person whom we pity. Yes, an insult hurts, but the only person it harms is the one who hurls it. If we can absorb an insult for the love of God, we will retain our peace. As St. Francis de Sales writes regarding how to respond to hurtful remarks, "Nothing breaks the force of a cannonball as well as wool."[27]

In Times of Anxiety 6

In *The Screwtape Letters,* a devil named Screwtape gives his nephew Wormwood the following advice on how to keep human beings from thinking about God. "There is nothing like anxiety for barricading a human's mind against the Enemy [God]. God wants humans to be concerned with what they do; our business is to keep them thinking about what will happen to them. Your patient [the soul that Wormwood is tempting] will have picked up the notion that he must submit with patience to the Enemy's will. What the Enemy means by this is that he should accept with patience the tribulation that has actually been dealt out to him, the present anxiety. It is to this that he is to say 'Thy will be done.' It is your business to see that your patient never thinks of the present fear as his appointed cross but only of the things he is afraid of. Real resignation is to present fear. And resignation to present and actual suffering, even where the suffering consists of fear is far easier to bear and is usually helped by this direct action."[28]

The anxiety that erects a barricade between our mind and God can be the very instrument that makes us aware of God's presence. When we consciously bear something for the love of God, we become conscious of the God for whom we bear it. The next time that you are anxious, don't pray that the anxiety goes away but rather for the strength to bear it and to continue loving your neighbor in spite of it. If you do so, you will feel a peace beyond understanding because within the swirl of your anxiety you will become aware of a still point — the presence of God.

The Vow of Stability

7

In *The Cloister Walk*, Kathleen Norris writes, "One monk, when asked about the diversity in his small community, said that there were people who can meditate all day and others who can't sit still for five minutes; monks who are scholars and those who are semiliterate; chatterboxes and those who emulate Calvin Coolidge with regard to speech. 'But,' he said, 'our biggest problem is that each man here had a mother who fried potatoes in a different way. Differences between individuals will either be absorbed when the community gathers to act as one or these communal activities become battle grounds.'"[29] We all recognize the truth of this statement. Most of the aggravations and irritations of daily life are the result of personality clashes and differences in individual preferences. No matter where we live, this is the human condition.

Benedictine monks and nuns take a vow of stability, the promise to live in a specific monastery for life. This vow contains the challenge of accepting life on its own terms. As Thomas Merton writes, by making the vow of stability "a monk renounces the vain hope of wandering off to find a perfect community."[30]

We cannot have peace and emotional stability until we let go of the illusionary belief that a place exists where everyone's mother fried potatoes the same way. But perfect communities do exist. They are found where everyone accepts that no one is perfect or ever will be.

Notes

[1] J. P. Decaussade, S. J., *Self-abandonment to Divine Providence*, trans. Algar Thorold (Springfield: Templegate, 1959), 152-3.

[2] John Milton, *Paradise Lost,* Bk. 1, line 254-5.

[3] J. P. Decaussade, Ibid., 435.

[4] *Letters of Wolfgang Amadeus Mozart*, selected and edited by Hans Mershmann, trans. M.M. Bozman (New York: Dover Publications, Inc., 1972), 233.

[5] William Shakespeare, *Henry V*, Act IV. Sc 3. l.76.

[6] *St. Thérèse of Lisieux: By Those Who Knew Her*, ed. and trans. Christopher O'Mahony (Dublin: Veritas Publications, 1975), 132.

[7] St. Thomas Aquinas, *Summa Theologiae*, Volume 34, trans. R. J. Batten O.P. (New York: McGraw-Hill, 1975), II-II, Q. 23, art. 2, 15.

[8] Pseudo-Dionyius, "The Divine Names," *in Pseudo Dionysius: The Complete Works*, trans. Colon Luibheid (New York: Paulist Press, 1987), 77.

[9] St. John of the Cross, "The Ascent of Mount Carmel," in The Collected Works of St. John of the Cross, trans. Kieran Kavanaugh, O.C.D. and Otilio Rodriguez, O.C.D. (Washington, D.C.: ICS Publications, 1991), 288.

[10] William Wordsworth, "Tintern Abbey," in *William Wordsworth*, ed. Stephan Gill (Oxford: Oxford University Press, 1984), 132.

[11] St. Thérèse of Lisieux, *Story of a Soul*, trans. John Clarke, O.C.D. (Washington, D.C.: ICS Publications, 1996), 221.

[12] John Henry Newman, "The Mind of Little Children," in Parochial and Plain Sermons, Vol. 2 (New York: Scribner, Welford & Co., 1868), 64.

[13] Marcus Aurelius, *Meditations*, trans. Maxwell Staniforth (Baltimore: Penguin Books, 1964), 115.

[14] William Blake, "Songs of Innocence," in *William Blake: The Complete Poems*, ed. Alicia Ostriker (New York: Penguin Books, 1988), 107.

[15] Oscar Wilde, "De Profundis," in *De Profundis and Other Writings* (New York: Penguin Books, 1987), 143.

[16] St. Augustine, *Soliloquies*, Kim Paffenroth, translator, Hyde Park, NY: New City Press, 2000.

[17] St. Thérèse of Lisieux, *Letters of St. Thérèse of Lisieux* Volume 1, trans. John Clarke, O.C.D. (Washington, D.C.: ICS Publications, 1982), 467.

[18] Gerard Manley Hopkins, "Letter to Robert Bridges, January 19, 1879. Quoted from *Letters from Saints to Sinners*, ed. John Cumming (New York: Crossroad Publishing Company, 1987), 21.

[19] St. Teresa of Avila, "The Way of Perfection," in *The Collected Works of St. Teresa of Avila:* Vol.2. trans Kieran Kavanaugh, O.C.D. and Otilio Rodriguez, O.C.D. (Washington, D.C.: 1980), 79-80.

[20] St. Francis de Sales, *Introduction to the Devout Life*, trans. Michael Day (Anthony Clarke: Wheathampstead, Hertfordshire, 1954), 94.

[21] Sr. Genevieve of the Holy Face (Celine Martin), *A memoir of my sister St. Thérèse*, trans. Carmelite Sisters of New York (New York: P.J. Kenedy & Sons, 1959), 61-2.

[22] St. Francis de Sales, Ibid., 115-116.

[23] Bill Wilson, *Twelve Steps and Twelve Traditions* (New York: Alcoholics Anonymous Publishing, 1981), 62.

[24] Francis Thompson, *"The Hound of Heaven,"* in *The Complete Poetical Works of Francis Thompson* (New York: Boni and Liveright, 1913), 93.

[25] Dante, *The Inferno*, trans. John Ciardi (New York: New American Library, 1982), 277.

[26] John Climacus, *The Ladder of Divine Ascent*, trans. Colm Luibheid and Norman Russell (New York: Paulist Press, 1982), 146 & 150.

[27] St. Francis de Sales, Ibid., 112.
[28] C.S. Lewis, *The Screwtape Letters* (New York: Macmillan Company, 1961), 29.
[29] Kathleen Norris, *The Cloister Walk* (New York: Riverhead Books, 1987), 21.
[30] Thomas Merton, *The Sign of Jonas* (New York: Harcourt, Brace & Company, 1953), 10.

Also available in the same series:

Three Minutes for the Soul
Reflections to Start the Day

Gerhard Bauer

72 pages
ISBN: 978-1-56548-275-3

Mary
Four Weeks with the Mother of Jesus

Edited by Wolfgang Bader and Stefan Liesenfeld

72 pages
ISBN: 978-1-56548-281-6

Pathways to God
Four Weeks on Faith, Hope and Charity

Robert F. Morneau

72 pages
ISBN 978-1-56548-286-9

In preparation:

Sister Earth
Ecology, Creation, and the Spirit

Dom Helder Camara

To order call 1-800-462-5980
or e-mail orders@newcitypress.com